THE NOT DEAD

"The lacuna between lyric and prose was addressed in *The Not Dead*, one of the bravest and most thoughtful broadcast reactions to the duty of remembrance."
A.A. Gill, *The Sunday Times*

"... a stunning technique. Rarely does poetry sound so natural, as easy in the mouth as it did here ... This was commemorative TV at its most vital."
Hermione Eyre, *The Independent On Sunday*

"It's bold, brave, beautiful television; it makes you think, it leaves you numb."
Sam Wollaston, *The Guardian*

"The award-winning combination of director Brian Hill and poet Simon Armitage explore the profound cost of fighting and killing through the stories of three men ... Armitage's poetry, delivered by the veterans, gives clarity to their pain and loss ..."
Daily Telegraph

"... the post-traumatic stress disorder of demobilised soldiers is a social issue that keeps raising its ugly head, but seldom has the case for the forgotten, still living war heroes been so touchingly put."
Rob Sharp, *The Independent On Sunday*

"*The Not Dead* is so moving, shaming and inspiring."
Ron Hanks, *The Independent*

"This is an incredibly moving film"
Emma Perry, *Time Out*

"A bleak, beautiful and blistering film ... one of the best films you will see all year."
Gareth McLean, *The Guardian*

"After all, this could have provided the basis of, say, a *Panorama* report on the national scandal of the way we treat the young men we send to fight our wars. Armitage's verse adds a special dimension — the emotional truth of the matter."
Gerard Gilbert, *The Independent*

"*The Not Dead* is uniquely impressive. In transmuting the stories of particular soldiers into the lyrical music of Simon Armitage's poems, something exceptional is achieved: the painful truth of lives damaged beyond help is made meaningful for the rest of us. We can only catch our breath and read them again and again."
Joan Bakewell

SIMON ARMITAGE

THE NOT DEAD

◆

POMONA

125/500

A Pomona Book

P - 015

Published by Pomona Books 2008
PO Box 50, Hebden Bridge, West Yorkshire HX7 8WA, England, UK
Telephone 01422 846900 · e-mail ursula@pomonauk.co.uk
www.pomonauk.co.uk

1

A CIP catalogue record for this book
is available from the British Library

ISBN 978-1-904-59018-7

ISBN 978-1-904-59019-4
[Special Edition]

Typeset in Monotype Centaur by Christian Brett at Bracketpress
Printed and bound in England by CPI Cox & Wyman, Reading RG1 8EX

For Robert Kirby

Introduction

The film *The Not Dead* was commissioned by Channel 4, produced by Century Films and broadcast on Remembrance Sunday 2007. It represents the seventh poetry/film collaboration between myself and director Brian Hill in which we've attempted to challenge the conventions of factual film-making, enhance the voices of participating characters and make memorable television. Although all of our films have been "documentaries", they have each involved some written or dramatised element, ranging from poetic voice-over to full-blown song lyrics. My role in *The Not Dead* was to listen to the statements of its contributors — soldiers, real people with true stories to tell — and turn their experiences into poems.

Around the time the film appeared, a number of newspaper articles asked why no contemporary war poetry was being written. Most of us read the War Poets at school. Some read the poetry of World War II, but for the majority it was the poetry of the Great War. Today, the poets of the trenches (Wilfred Owen, Siegfried Sassoon, Rupert Brooke, Robert Graves, Ivor Gurney and others) continue to hold their place within the canon of English literature and the education syllabus, and for good reason. Put crudely, poetry at its best says something about the human condition, often in relation to death, and the poets of WWI were serious writers operating at the very limit of human experience, sending back first-hand literary reports. It's difficult to imagine an equivalent situation ever occurring again, at least in the West. Most of the poets I know would think twice before setting a mouse-trap, let alone enlisting for active service, and I don't have the subscription figures in front of me but I'd guess that readership of *Poetry Review* amongst Her Majesty's Armed Forces is pretty low. True, Brian Turner, the American soldier with the creative writing MA, published a volume of war poetry which goes far beyond the hobbyist poetry that most people write at some time in their lives, especially to express sadness or loss, but he is the exception who proves the rule.

However, literary poets *are* writing war poetry today, it's just a question of knowing where to look for it, and recognising it when it is found. Warfare has changed and so has poetry. It could be argued, for instance, that in an art-form where context is sometimes just as important as content, the permanent backdrop of our current military situation makes almost *every* poem a war poem. In the same way, a single mention of a blood-orange sky or even a shooting star might alert the careful reader to the true metaphorical significance of a poem, even if that poem appeared, at first glance, to be about an empty desert at sunset. Warfare has echoed constantly through contemporary Irish poetry. Of the British, James Fenton, Michael Symmons Roberts, David Harsent, Glyn Maxwell, Peter Reading and Jo Shapcott to name but a few have all addressed war, sometimes through the long, lingering shadows of previous campaigns. Others have met war head-on, none more directly than Tony Harrison with his Gulf War poems "Initial Illumination" and "A Cold Coming".

The Not Dead was a war film. It was about returning soldiers, and in keeping with the literary tradition, the mode of expression was verse. There were three main participants in the film. Cliff was a veteran of the Malaya Emergency, Eddie served in Bosnia and Rob fought in Basra. Like Owen and Sassoon before them, they all suffered from what has come to be known as Post-Traumatic Stress Disorder, a version of what was previously referred to as shell-shock. Along with other soldiers we interviewed for the film, it was appalling to hear how little help these men had received. Many of the younger servicemen had turned to drink and drugs to blot out images of war, and a significant number had attempted suicide.

For some of the men, being in the film meant re-living their worst nightmares; most of the poems I wrote revolved around a key "flash-back" scene, requiring each soldier to re-visit the very incident he was desperately hoping to forget. On this point, it is curious to note how conventional psychological help has proved largely ineffective with PTSD. Most therapy involves dealing with issues, then moving on. But for traumatised soldiers, the harrowing images and accompanying feelings persist, in some cases for a lifetime. It's more a case of learning how to live with them. Rob was part of an attack on a bank in which an Iraqi man was shot as he burst through the doors. Rob doesn't say if he fired the fatal round, but in the days that followed, while on patrol, he had to walk across the dead-man's "blood-shadow" on several occasions. Like many serviceman, being a soldier had been Rob's dream from boyhood. To this day he's patriotic, nationalistic even, but the only Albion he'll fight for now is his beloved West Brom. As he says in the film, he was fully prepared for battle, but not prepared at all for coming home. Since absconding, his life has followed an all too familiar pattern of insomnia, alcoholism, drug abuse, homelessness, violence and crime. He feels damaged and helpless, but most of all he feels forgotten, or worse, ignored.

Cliff's feelings of guilt and shame have only increased with age and the pictures in his head are as clear today as they were half a century ago. At 75 he can't talk about the jungle ambush he was involved in without tears rolling down his face, and when it comes to speaking of his fellow soldiers who died in the attack, he can barely get the words out of his mouth. Time, often thought of as the great healer, has not done anything to diminish his sense of grief; Cliff is a man wearied and condemned by memories.

Of all three servicemen, Eddie appeared to have suffered the most, despite the fact he was serving in Bosnia as UN Peacekeeper, wearing a "blue lid." A born soldier, he expected to shoot and be shot at — that's what he was trained for. Instead, he lifted the barrier at the check-point to wave through the death squads. A couple of days later he'd be a member of the party that went in to witness the horror and clean up the mess. He describes, at one stage, a pregnant woman tied to a tree, cut open, with her dead, unborn baby hanging from her womb. There are other things he won't describe, he says, because they are worse. After returning home, to try and cure his nerves and overcome his paranoid reaction to loud bangs, he took a revolver into the middle of a field and fired several blank rounds against his head. He also tried to hang himself from a tree.

I wasn't present when the characters in the film read their pieces to camera, but it couldn't have been easy for them. The Army is a MAN'S WORLD. Trained soldiers are not encouraged to open their hearts, and confessing feelings of vulnerability, insecurity and fear on national television constitutes, in my view, a supreme act of bravery. Rob can hardly lift his face to the camera. Cliff seems to be permanently on the point of collapse. Invited to make himself comfortable, Eddie half-demolished the room he was filmed in, kicking at doors and furniture until it looked like the scene of some unspeakable Bosnian massacre. Then he was ready to start. And the last word came not from a man but from the voice of Laura, Eddie's wife. Tracing the scar of a bullet that took away part of her husband's face before pin-balling through his body, she describes the slow and painful process of trying to reach him, touch him, love him, and make him human again. In the film, the scene provides an obvious, ironic contrast with Britain itself, its majors and generals bemused, irritated and embarrassed by these broken men, the mother country washing her hands of those soldiers who escaped death only to return home as "untouchables," as haunting and haunted ghosts.

◆

There are nine poems in this book. "Remains" and "Albion" were written for Rob. "The Black Swans" and "Scarecrows" were written for Eddie. "The Manhunt" was written for Laura. "Warriors" was written for Scott, a Gulf War veteran who did not appear in the final film. "The Malaya Emergency" and "The Parting Shot" were written for Cliff. The title poem, written to summarise the sentiments of all the returning combatants who participated, was recited in the film by Rob, Eddie and Cliff. Thanks are hereby paid to all those who agreed to take part in this project, and also to Combat Stress, the ex-services mental welfare society, for their advice and support.

The Not Dead

◆

We are the not dead.
In battle, life would not say goodbye to us.
And crack-shot snipers seemed to turn a blind eye to us.
And even though guns and grenades let fly at us
we somehow survived.

We are the not dead.
When we were young and fully alive for her,
we worshipped Britannia.
We the undersigned
put our names on the line for her.
From the day we were born we were loaded and primed for her.
Prepared as we were, though, to lie down and die for her,
we somehow survived.

So why did she cheat on us?
Didn't we come running when she most needed us?
When tub-thumping preachers
and bullet-brained leaders
gave solemn oaths and stirring speeches
then fisted the air and pointed eastwards,
didn't we turn our backs on our nearest and dearest?
From runways and slipways Britannia cheered us,
but returning home refused to meet us,
sent out a crowd of back-biting jeerers
and mealy-mouth sneerers.
Two-timing, two-faced Britannia deceived us.

We are morbidly ill.
Soldiers with nothing but time to kill,
we idle now in everyday clothes and ordinary towns,
blowing up, breaking down.
If we dive for cover or wake in a heap,
Britannia, from horseback, now crosses the street
or looks right through us.
We seem changed and ghostly to those who knew us.
The country which flew the red white and blue for us
now shows her true colours.
We are the not-dead.
Neither happy and proud
with a bar-code of medals across the heart
nor laid in a box and draped in a flag,
we wander this no-man's land instead,
creatures of different stripe – the awkward, unwanted, unlovable type –
haunted with fear and guilt,
wounded in spirit and mind.

So what shall we do with the not dead and all of his kind?

The Black Swans

◆

Through a panel of glass in the back of the wagon
the country went past. You clean your weapon,
make camp, drive around, stand guard, stand down.
Sit with a gun in your hand and your thumb up your arse.
Or you try to get shot at – just for a laugh.

Nineteen, fighting the boredom, wearing a blue lid.
Then one day the kid who gets smokes for the lads
walks into the woods and never comes back.
Then one day the Black Swans drive by in a van –
a death squad of Bennies in bobble hats, wielding Kalashnikovs,
smirking, running their fingers across their throats.
Not to be checked or blocked. A law unto themselves.

Walk in the valley. Walk in the shadow of death
in the wake of the Black Swans, treading the scorched earth.
Houses trashed and torched. In a back yard
a cloud of bluebottles hides a beheaded dog.
This woman won't talk, standing there open-mouthed,
tied to a tree, sliced from north to south.
In the town square, a million black-eyed bullet-holes stare
and stare. Crows lift from the mosque. Behind the school,
flesh-smoke – sweet as incense – rises and hangs
over mounds of soil planted with feet and hands.

Albion

◆

I was a boy soldier, back when grenades were pine cones
and guns were sticks.

I played Churchill's speeches, fought on the beaches as Vera Lynn
sang from the white cliffs,

and I dreamed the dream of a hero's welcome, of flags and bunting
lining the streets,

of drinking for free in every bar, of beautiful women with open arms
and white cotton sheets.

But instead of klaxons and Union Jacks came sticking plasters
to cover the cracks,

and ibuprofen to ease the mind. Without blood or scars or a missing leg
you're swinging the lead;

without entry wounds and exit wounds or burns to the face
you're just soft in the head,

and the British Army isn't the place for a lying bastard
or basket case.

What I did, I did for St George and for England and God;
now I sleep in sweat,

sleighing the dragon or training the crosshairs on mum and dad
and shooting them dead.

Distraction helps. The beast stalks in the day, kept back by the noise and the light,

but after the action, emptiness falls on the Hawthorns and darkness stirs. Then cometh the night.

Remains

◆

On another occasion, we get sent out
to tackle looters raiding a bank.
And one of them legs it up the road,
probably armed, possibly not.

Well myself and somebody else and somebody else
are all of the same mind,
so all three of us open fire.
Three of a kind all letting fly, and I swear

I see every round as it rips through his life –
I see broad daylight on the other side.
So we've hit this looter a dozen times
and he's there on the ground, sort of inside out,

pain itself, the image of agony.
One of my mates goes by
and tosses his guts back into his body.
Then he's carted off in the back of a lorry.

End of story, except not really.
His blood-shadow stays on the street, and out on patrol
I walk right over it week after week.
Then I'm home on leave. But I blink

and he bursts again through the doors of the bank.
Sleep, and he's probably armed, possibly not.
Dream, and he's torn apart by a dozen rounds.
And the drink and the drugs won't flush him out –

he's here in my head when I close my eyes,
dug in behind enemy lines,
not left for dead in some distant, sun-stunned, sand-smothered land
or six-feet-under in desert sand,

but near to the knuckle, here and now,
his bloody life in my bloody hands.

Warriors

◆

It's just one massive ditch, the border with Kuwait,
and once over the bun-line the heart bounces and kicks,
expecting fury unleashed, the mother of all fights,
a million attackers in sandals all armed to the teeth.
But there's only sand and some goat-boy walking his herd.
The gun-turret spins a full 360 degrees – like an owl's head.

Rumble onward all night till you're just about cooked.
The section commander gets out for a piss and almost loses his cock.
Crunch over something brittle, plough through something soft,
rounds pinging the metal like jet-propelled wasps,
the Warrior slewing and spinning. It roars forward, then stops.
Range 410 miles, road speed 46 miles per hour – tops.

Banged up for nine hours in half-light and slow heat,
but it's only the last thirty seconds that truly count,
before the lid comes off. As the last moments are dealt out
some guys scream and shout, bringing their blood to the boil;
others stare into friends' eyes, right to the back of the skull.
Deployment is via a hydraulic door in the hull.

What happens thereafter, either I won't say, or can't.
To survive, good infantrymen keep their emotions locked
and imaginations screwed shut. If not, the door of the truck
becomes like the back of an old-fashioned camera: open it up
and the sun floods in, blazes the film, and you're fucked.
A Rolls Royce V8 Condor engine grinds sand in its guts.

Scarecrows

♦

Life wants to live, and nature will lift and restore
the fallen and broken.
Nevertheless, a hose-pipe snakes through the vehicle door,
and you sit there, son, with the engine purring,
not to be woken,
breathing the fumes till the world stops turning.

They'll be harvesting now in parts of the Balkans,
carts piled high,
patches of earth unpredictably fertile. Fruitful.
From blister-packs and childproof bottles
you count out the pills,
swilling them down with vodka and Redbull.

In the butcher's window, a side of beef
is precisely a corpse.
A slash to the wrists would be painless and quick
if the blade was keen and the hand held steady,
but you flinch from the thought,
having witnessed so much of your blood already.

The trees are waiting, heaven sent. Sling a rope
from a lime or an oak –
(how good does it feel, the noose on the throat?) –
and swing from a branch, but the branch won't hold.
Then wake in sweat
with your hands in a knot around Laura's neck.

A birthday balloon goes off like a bomb
and a car backfires.
But you, you're a son of the soil, are you not?
So take up your gun
and shoot yourself stupid, blank after blank,
over and over again till the hands don't shake,
and the nerves don't *feel*,
and the crows have risen and flapped from the ploughed field.

The Malaya Emergency

◆

One road in, one road out.
A world away from a bricklayer's yard,
from Manchester's oily ship canal
to a tented camp on a river bank.
River runs deep. River runs dark.

One road there, one road back.
Leaf-light dapples a mountain track.
Then all-out attack.
Buds like bullets, flowers like flack.
River runs thick, river runs fast.

Me and Lomas and Polish John.
We sat and thought.
Whispered and smoked.
Men without rank, men on their own.
One road out, one road home . . .

so we drove back into the killing zone,
just drove right into the killing zone,
river still rolling, turning its stones,
mates I'd drank and laughed and joked with,
mates I'd effed and jeffed and smoked with
are butchered now and their shirts are burning,
river still writhing, river still turning,

Joe with his eye shot out of his head,
(He'll live for now but meet his end
in a Manchester doorway, begging for bread),
river runs black, river runs red,
some boy wailing his mother's name,
Tommy asleep with a hole in his brain . . .
I found his killer and shot him dead,
tossed him onto a barbed wire fence,
taught him a lesson, left him to rot.

Job done.
Till thirty years on,
when the dead, like the drowned, float up to top.

One road out, one road in.
And all for what – rubber and tin.
A can of beans, a bicycle tyre.
A river in flames, a river on fire.
A bicycle tyre and a can of beans
and a river that streams and streams and streams.

The Parting Shot

◆

So five graves, like long evening shadows, are dug,
and the five coffins wait in line, varnished and squared off,
and the firing party aims for the distance and fires,
and all are starched and suited and booted and buttoned up.

Then ramrod straight, under the shade of a tree,
the boy-bugler raises a golden horn to his lips,
and calls to his dead friends with his living breath.
And the tune never wavers or breaks,
but now tears roll from his eyes,
tears which fall from his face and bloom
on his ironed green shirt like two dark wounds.

Then the world swims and drowns in everyone else's eyes too.

The Manhunt

◆

After the first phase,
after passionate nights and intimate days,

only then would he let me trace
the frozen river which ran through his face,

only then would he let me explore
the blown hinge of his lower jaw,

and handle and hold
the damaged, porcelain collar-bone,

and mind and attend
the fractured rudder of shoulder-blade,

and finger and thumb
the parachute silk of his punctured lung.

Only then could I bind the struts
and climb the rungs of his broken ribs,

and feel the hurt
of his grazed heart.

Skirting along,
only then could I picture the scan,

the foetus of metal beneath his chest
where the bullet had finally come to rest.

Then I widened the search,
traced the scarring back to its source

to a sweating, unexploded mine
buried deep in his mind, around which

every nerve in his body had tightened and closed.
Then, and only then, did I come close.

Pomona is a wholly independent publisher dedicated to bringing before the public the work of prodigiously talented writers. Tell your friends. Our books can be purchased on-line at: www.pomonauk.co.uk

Pomoma backlist